Big and Small Homes for All

by Joanne Mattern

MODERN CURRICULUM PRESS
Pearson Learning Group

Birds build all kinds of nests!

Some are big. Some are small. Some are on high branches. Some are underground burrows.

A bird lays its eggs in a nest. A nest keeps the eggs safe. A bird builds its nest using things it finds close by.

Gulls use rocks they find on the shore. Birds in the woods use grasses, leaves, and twigs. City birds even use string and paper!

A robin carries everything she needs to make her nest. She makes a pile of sticks and grass. Then she walks on the pile to make it flat.

The robin uses mud to stick her nest together. Then she pushes her body into the pile. She twists and turns. Soon the nest looks like a bowl. The shape of the nest keeps the eggs from falling out.

Weaver birds live in Africa and Asia. They spend time searching for special grasses. The weaver bird makes a knotted ring of grass. It hangs the ring from a tree. Then it uses its beak like a sewing needle. It weaves grass in and out, around and around.

When the weaver bird's nest is done, it is strong and waterproof. Some weaver bird nests have a long tunnel. This tunnel keeps snakes from getting into the nest and eating the baby chicks.

Many birds build nests out of mud. This ovenbird builds its nest out of muddy clay. It builds its nest in the winter, when the clay is soft and wet. In the spring, the hot sun dries the nest. Then the nest is hard and strong.

A flamingo's nest looks like a mud pot! The flamingo picks up mud in its beak. Then it drops the mud into a pile. It uses its webbed feet to press the mud into a tall cone.

Large groups of barn swallows live in barns and other buildings. Swallows spend time searching for mud. They carry the mud into a barn. They stick the mud to a wall. Then they stick pieces of straw to the mud. It takes about a week for the swallows to build their nests.

Hornbills build strange nests. The female hornbill finds a hole in a tree.

She seals herself inside the hole with mud. She stays inside the nest until her eggs hatch and her chicks are old enough to fly. The male hornbill passes food to the family through a small hole.

Sparrows are small birds. They can build their nests in small places, like inside this letter. Sometimes a sparrow even builds a nest inside a traffic light. Maybe the heat from the light keeps the eggs warm until they hatch.

A woodpecker eats insects that live in trees. The woodpecker uses its strong beak to drill a nest in the tree. It makes its nest close to its food. It uses wood chips and sawdust to make the inside of the nest soft and warm.

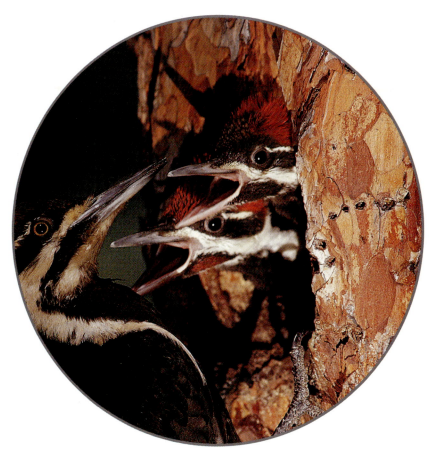

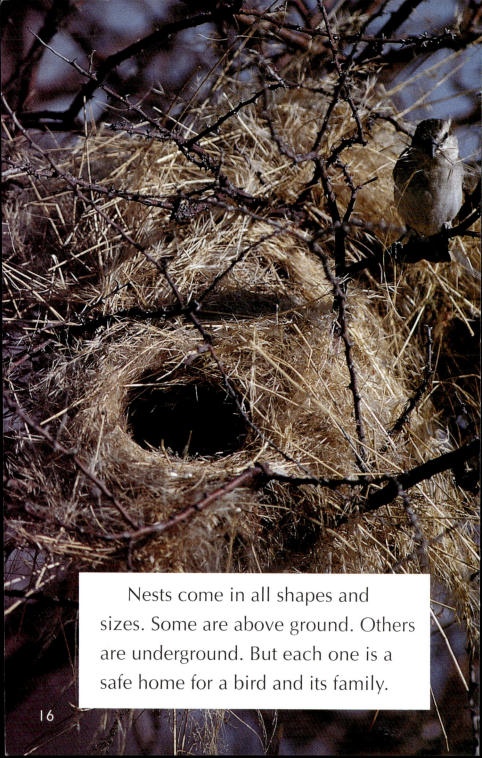

Nests come in all shapes and sizes. Some are above ground. Others are underground. But each one is a safe home for a bird and its family.